Wakeful night

a structured reflection on loss and illumination

NICOLE SKIBOLA

dottir press

NEW YORK CITY

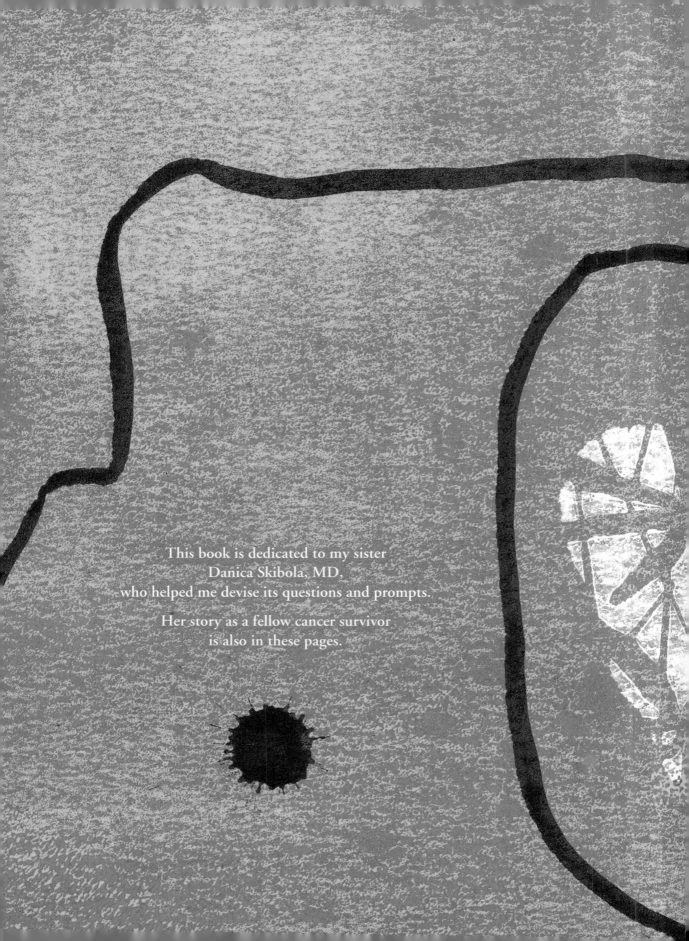

This book is dedicated to my sister
Danica Skibola, MD,
who helped me devise its questions and prompts.

Her story as a fellow cancer survivor
is also in these pages.

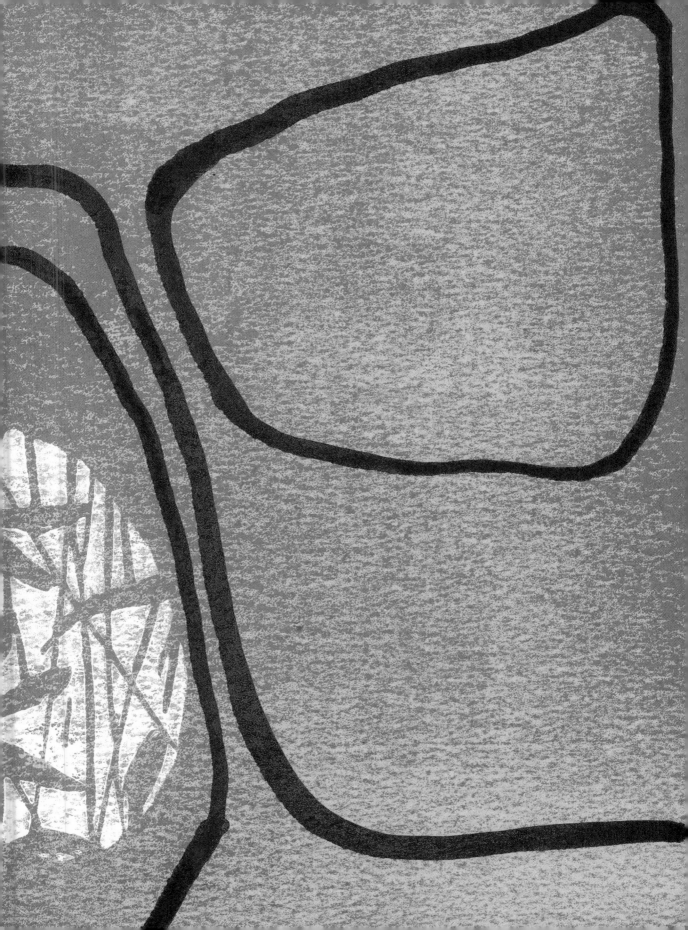

Introduction

I receive a diagnosis for a rare endometrial cancer. I am thirty-two. The words drip from the mouth of my doctor, forever suspended in time. A race begins to understand, to save eggs, to mourn the loss of my reproductive organs, to be angry, to be okay.

My bodily survival is burdened with a crushing pressure to continue as the person I am before my illness. *Things will be back to normal soon*, a nurse chirps, slipping in an IV. *Be happy you're alive*, a friend tells me as I sob uncontrollably over a video chat. I am guilty for my sorrow. No one, I remind myself, wants to hear about my reorganized peritoneal cavity or spiraling mental instability. I perform normalcy like a champ. I expertly evade my own emptiness and rage.

❧

The weeks leading up to surgery to remove my uterus, ovaries, and fallopian tubes contain a daily pilgrimage. Before dawn, I take a bus to a subway and walk almost a mile to a hospital at the edge of Manhattan. In a dark, cube-sized room, I remove my pants and winter layers, and then wait in stirrups for a lubricated wand to enter. My eyes hold the sonogram screen with intensity, willing the pixelated gray to reveal signs of follicular life. My abdomen is raw and bloated; the sleeves of every sweater are marked with the tracks of saline and mucous, evidence of a month-long goodbye.

My pregnant sister flies out from California for my first injections. She peppers my fertility doctor with questions I am unable to ask and fills out my medical forms for me so that I don't have to give my date of birth again and again and again. I am taking a medical risk with an egg retrieval, injecting hormones into my cancer-ridden pelvis. My mother and my partner beg me not to do it, but I see *her*: the little girl I am supposed to have.

❧

I wake from a long drugged sleep. The dim hospital room is filled with muffled whispers, nervous sighs, hands tending to IVs and monitors. Almost as quickly as I blink into the beige walls and square paneled ceiling of hospital consciousness, I am

overtaken by the quiet shadow: grief. It is immediate, suffocating, and primordial. An image emerges in my mind's eye, body parts seeping down the sterile walls, their fluid collecting in cracks between plastic molding and speckled linoleum floor.

I make a drawing of this hospital room. It begins midway up the walls where the lonely pole of a water bag hangs. A long, wall-mounted light fixture hovers over an invisible patient bed. The walls are covered with hand-drawn wallpaper—a continuous pattern of a uterus, ovaries, and fallopian tubes—distorted backward in perspective on either sidewall. At the crease where the walls meet the ceiling, a pool of watery red paint bleeds down each surface until it runs clear toward the bottom row of visible organs.

⁓

On my thirty-third birthday, I tell my boyfriend: *I want to be engaged by the end of the year*. I am tumbling, out of control, desperate for something to break my fall into the subaquatic horizon. *It's too much* he tries to tell me, not so much in words but by cowardly fading away. *It's okay*, I tell him, pretending to be an understanding girlfriend. This is her final chapter; the end of Nicole before cancer.

⁓

With a cancer diagnosis, there are physical losses—breasts, colons, parts of lungs and legs. These body parts are considered in clinical terms and at some point they are labeled *excess*—diseased tissue to be hastily dumped in a biohazard bin. In reality, each physical piece of self is encoded with story and experience; each body part has its own memory.

I am aware of everything that I've lost with a few snips. I exchanged my life for part of my death. In her 2014 memoir, *Ghostbelly,* Elizabeth Heineman recounts her child's stillbirth and how a kind mortician allowed her to take home her son's body so that she could spend time with her baby before he was buried. She was able to grieve as a mother, to say goodbye in a ritualistic way not commonly supported in our society.

I think about taking home my own uterus, ovaries, and fallopian tubes.

I spend the weeks leading up to the surgery with my hands constantly on my pelvis, willing that sacred energy to remain inside of me, somehow. Those particular organs defined my identity as a woman for my entire conscious life, in pleasure, pain, and possibility. A dear acupuncturist friend teaches me of the *yin* in eastern medicine—*the female energy that persists*. The *yin* can never be surgically removed, I learn, just as the energy of a lost infant will never be banished with a physical burial. We are more than the mere sum of our parts.

My egg retrieval is, by all accounts, unsuccessful. The doctors overstimulate me, hoping to bolster my fertility in that small window, and the gamble fails. Watching pulses of ovaries and follicles (a dash of one large ova) on that tiny screen is the closest I will ever come to the wonder of spawning life. It is my final childbearing adagio. That little girl I keep seeing, it turns out, is me. Me: soon to be reborn in a way that those of us who have come close to death understand.

❧

Or maybe this ghost child will enter my life in another, circuitous, serendipitous way.

❧

Some mornings I wake up conscious of a parallel future I will never know as a woman. Attached to this heaviness are still-recent memories of loss and heartbreak. On this kind of day, I'm desperate to find the ocean.

In winter, I walk alongside freezing water, over sand cascading into tiny dunes leaning in the direction of the tidal winds. In the summer, my hunger to escape into the ocean is the most primal. I crash into the collapsing chop; I plunge into the aquatic night below.

Navigating the ocean is a game of submission and pugnacity, and I wildly flipper my feet until the foam is replaced with black stillness. I undulate in swells of water, give in to the heartbeat of the ruthless ocean. Swimming skill is not always associated with survival, and anyone could drown here, sink to a place where there is no sense of end or beginning, equilibrate with the earthly version of outer space. I imagine the ocean's horizon hovering over ancient sand and whisper to myself: *the wreck and not the story of the wreck*—words from my favorite poem, *Diving into the Wreck* by Adrienne Rich.

In my wreck I find my second survival, this time a spiritual one. Losing so much makes space to grow; being close to death violently peels away my story.

❧

The new story starts like this: On a freezing day in January, I stagger out of the Manhattan office building of the start-up where I work, place one hand against a freshly pine-mulched planter, and violently vomit what feels like every remnant of myself. Tears stream down my cheeks. Simultaneously, I weep and wretch and feebly apologize to business people buzzing by on their way to lunch meetings.

I concede defeat. I stop feigning that I am okay. I retreat to my empty childhood home in the hills of northern California. After many weeks of complete solitude, I

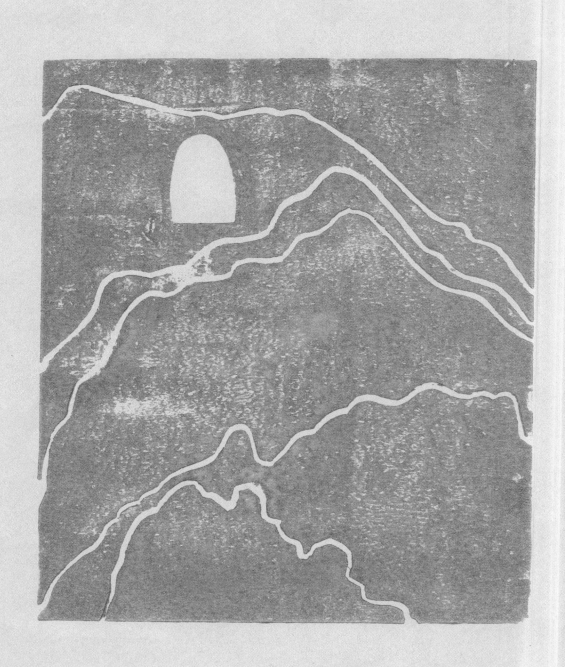

join a writer's group. It's a warm sunny afternoon. In the group are artists and writers who make work about death and stillbirths and personal trauma; the work is raw and stunningly beautiful. I feel a palpable sense of permission *to go there*, to give the middle finger to the Greek chorus chiming that sadness and honoring loss is a detrimental form of *hanging on*.

My early pieces are rough. I recount the same story over and over again—my organs, my partner leaving, the cancer rage. Then come the drawings—endless drawings of my life over the past few months. Some of the details are imagined, like pink tissue-y organs floating in darkness like sea anemones. Others are real, like the lonely shipping cranes I walk to at night. I sink into the losses, sometimes for days, as I write and draw the story of cancer in my life. Slowly, I identify a hunger—the creative emptiness that had gnawed away at my insides for years.

These writings and drawings become an illustrated memoir called *Nightflower*. My personal wreck is still painful, but it begins to feel malleable, a tool I can use to explore the person I am in the wake of loss. In this arc of anger, mourning, and acceptance, I experience an awakening. Facing the waves takes death-defying courage, but diving below the water's surface into the ribs of the wreck is how I become an artist.

Cancer, like any loss, is not a stand-alone event. There are disappointments, secondary losses, and questions that shake all assumptions of identity. (I could have limped away wounded, but the spiritual death of heartbreak and betrayal was the passageway to the person writing this introduction.) Grief is a deeply tangled, messy creature and in its folds is the heart's immense capacity to regenerate.

The more I draw and write, the more I grasp the deep human desire to share our stories. Stories honor grace and courage in the face of calamity. Outcome is irrelevant. Heroism is our capacity to see and feel.

❧

This journal is a structured guide to explore your own wreck; to honor your personal disaster. Stories can take any form, and stories in multiple forms are the most powerful. As you use this guide, remind yourself that there are no rules—there is no good or bad, no standard to which you must conform. Your story can be poems, dances, drawings, or songs. It can be shared or it can be yours alone forever.

Here is a wish: May you find the ocean. May you write the words to your own story. May you discover the beauty in what remains and the person you will become as you explore your own wakeful night.

—NS

Whether you leave this earth tomorrow
or live for fifty more years, who is this book for?

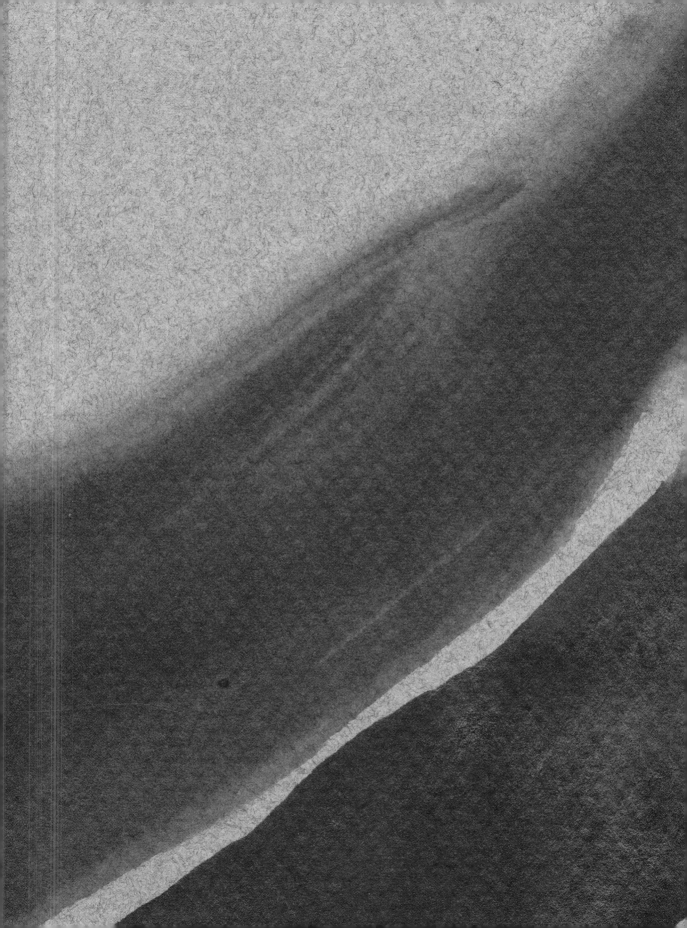

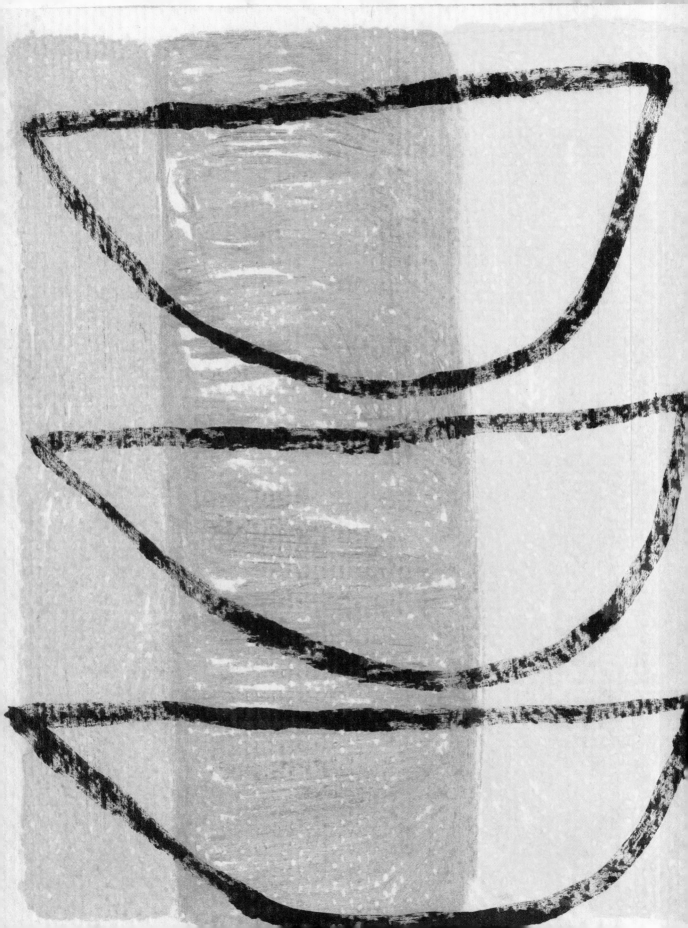

Who are you?

Think back to a favorite childhood memory.

Where were you?
Who were you with?
What were you wearing?
What were you doing?

How are you different from that kid now?

How are you the same?

Name or depict something you've created of which you are proud.

Describe any doubt that surrounded the creation of this thing
and the critic that still nags at you when you think about it.

Now write *I am an artist* ten times on this page of paper.
Keep right on writing it if you need to.

If you don't believe it, guess what?

All humans are artists.

Where is your inner artist right now?

Sitting shyly in the corner? Hiding in the closet?
Dancing in the middle of the room?

What does your inner artist look like?
What is your inner artist doing?

Give your inner artist permission to do
whatever the #$% it wants to do right now.

(Scream! Cry! Tear up a medical bill!
Throw a pillow! Dance on your bed!)

Repeat as often as possible.

What was your first thought when you were diagnosed?

Break it down.

Was it a fear of not having done enough?
Anticipation of hurting someone you love?
Dread about death or pain?

Focus on the emotion that thought evokes.
Love? Ambition? Fear? Anger?

Write about it.

Think of a color and shape this emotion elicits.

Draw it.

Develop this thought into a
recognizable object, animal, or place.
Use both pages.

Think about who you were before your diagnosis.

Remember what you cared about most,
what you did for fun, and what you took for granted.

Make five symbols or images that depict your former life.

Circle the ones you want to take with you.

Underline the ones you are prepared to leave behind.

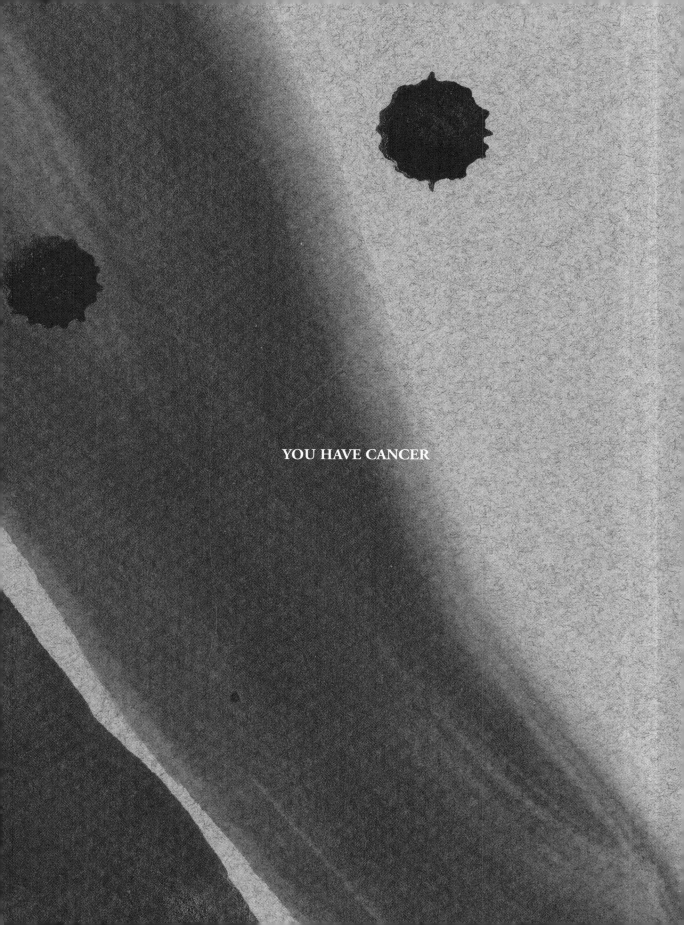

What did these words do to your body when you first heard them?
What did these words look and feel like?

In what ways have you resisted your life changing?

How has this resistance helped you?

How has it held you back?

Are there any forms of resistance you could release?

Rituals are a powerful way
to invite change,
prepare for a new
beginning,
say goodbye.

Can you think of a ritual
that would support you in
letting go of something?
(Maybe it's burning words
on a piece of paper,
throwing something
in the ocean, or
donating an object or
piece of clothing.)

Describe your ritual in detail.

Where will you go? Would you bring an object with you?
What time of day must it be? What do you have to do to prepare for this ritual?
Can you begin to plan this ritual?

What is your greatest fear?

Draw something that symbolizes the fear.

What does your inner artist say to this fear?

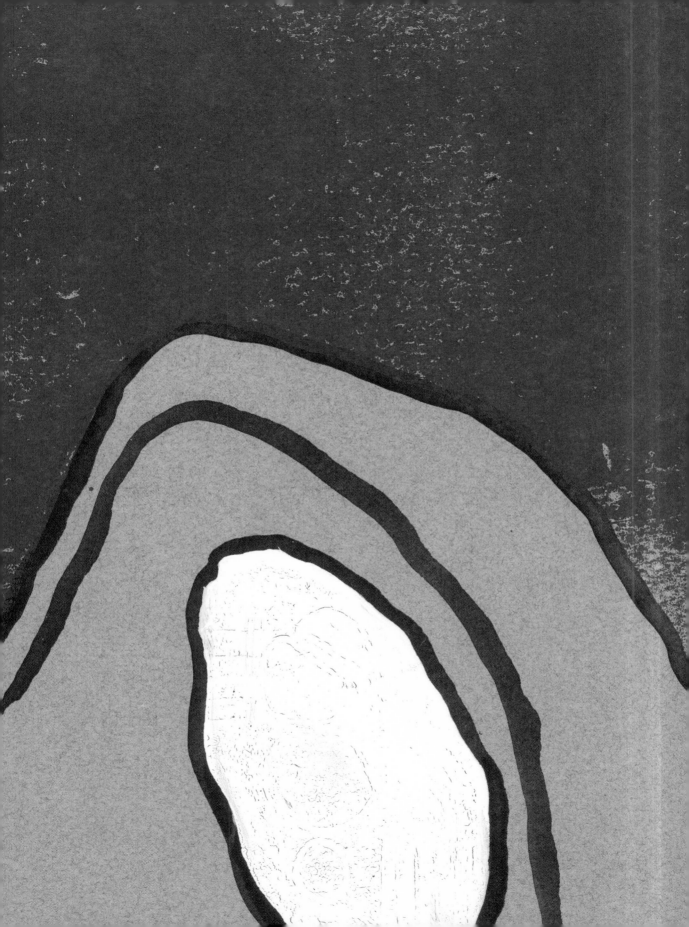

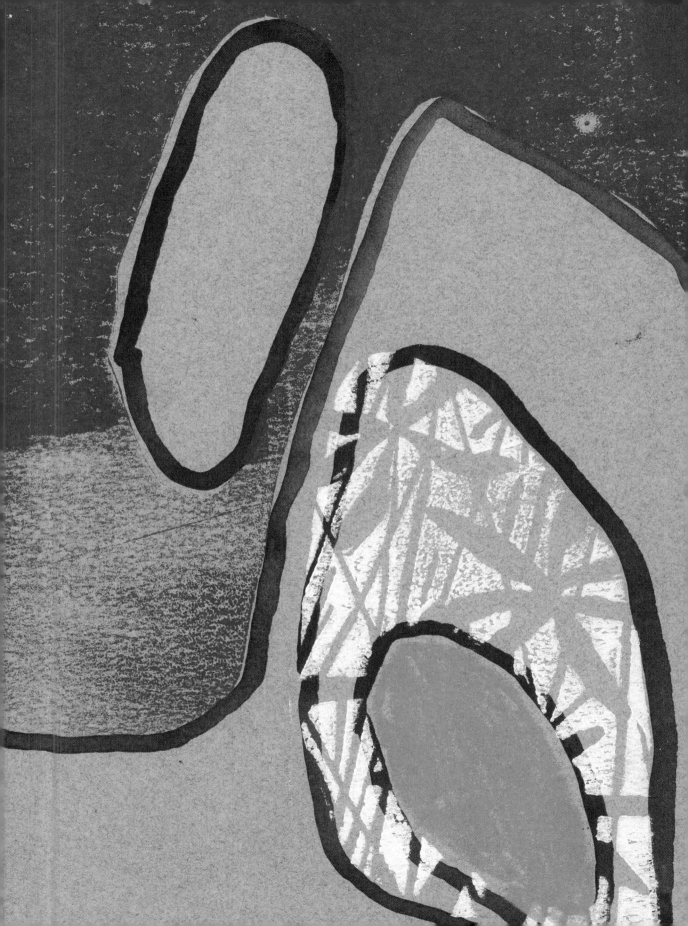

Make a self-portrait that represents this present moment.
It can be textures, colors, or shapes.
You can use collage or any media you want.

How does this self-portrait make you feel?
How might this portrait be different next year? In two years?

Write about it.

What was the hardest moment since diagnosis?

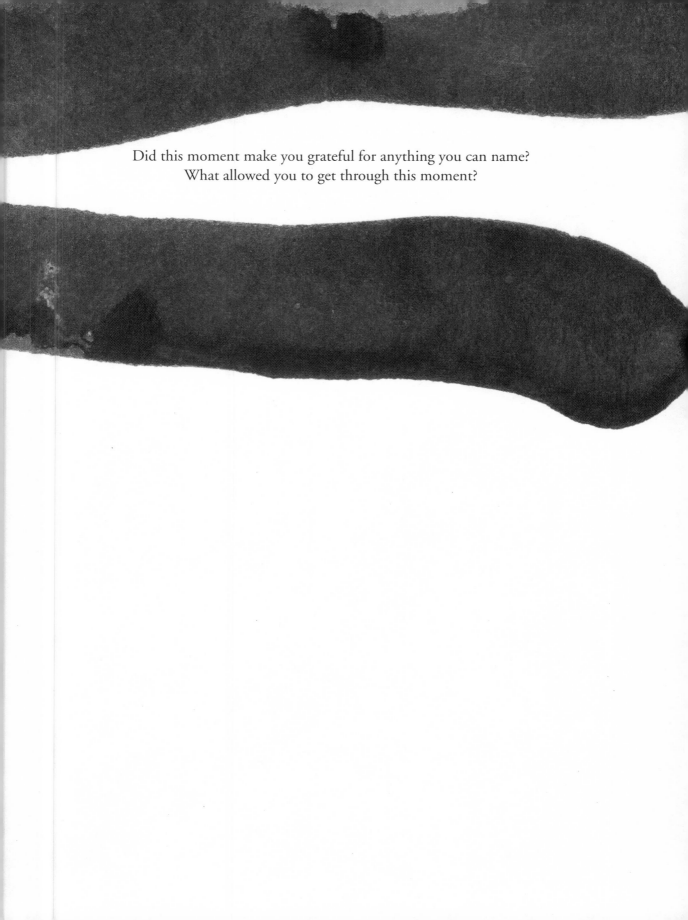

Did this moment make you grateful for anything you can name?
What allowed you to get through this moment?

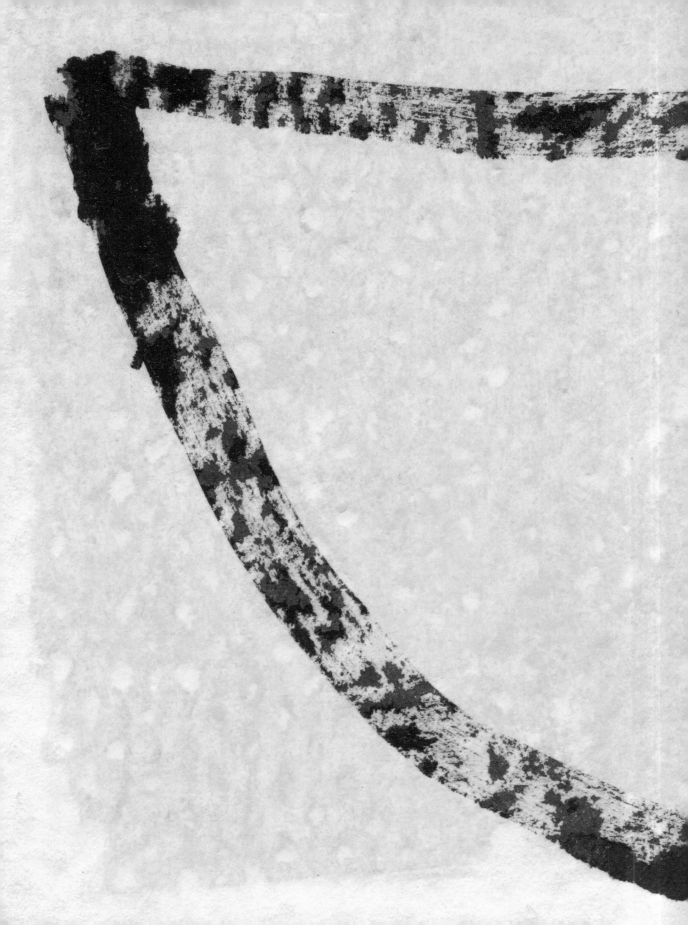

Write a letter to someone you love.

What would this person you love write back to you?
Do you think they see you differently than you see yourself right now?

How is your life changed forever by cancer?

One summer night shortly after my diagnosis,
I was riding my bike with my best friend.

As dusk burst across the balmy sky,
the tiny bodies of fireflies floated past us.
That moment was very emotional for me;
I realized suddenly
that the way I felt and saw the world
was irrevocably different.

Have you had one of those moments?

If you haven't yet, look for it. You'll find one.

If you had to describe one of these moments as a symbol, what would it be?

A treasure chest? An ocean? The Grand Canyon?

Draw it. It can be anything.

What is your greatest heartbreak associated with illness?

Now, pull apart the heartbreak to expose its veins of love, reverence, beauty, and gratitude.

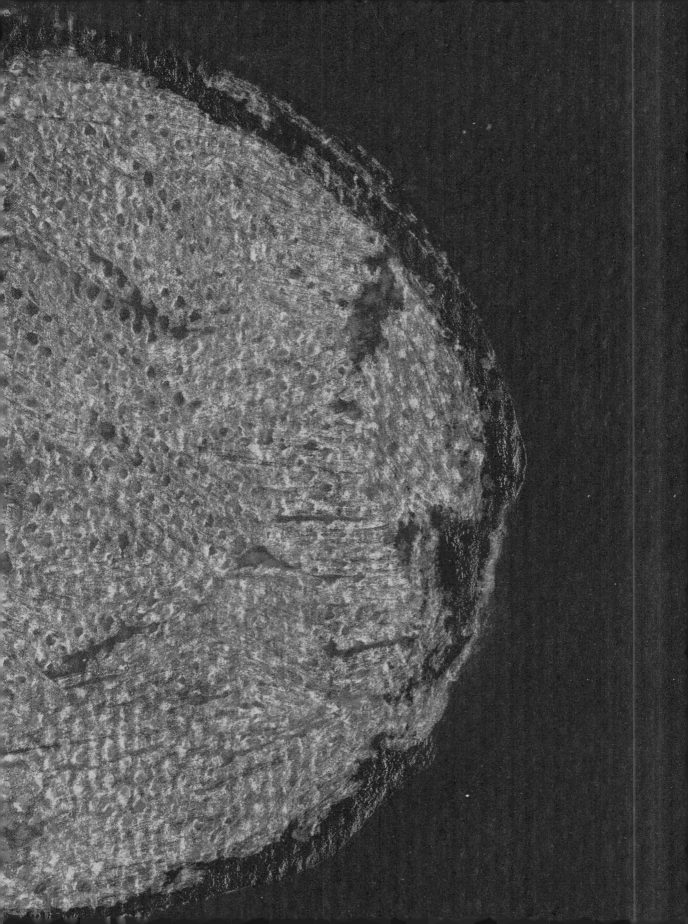

Draw some of the treasures in your life
that pierce the darkness of illness and loss.

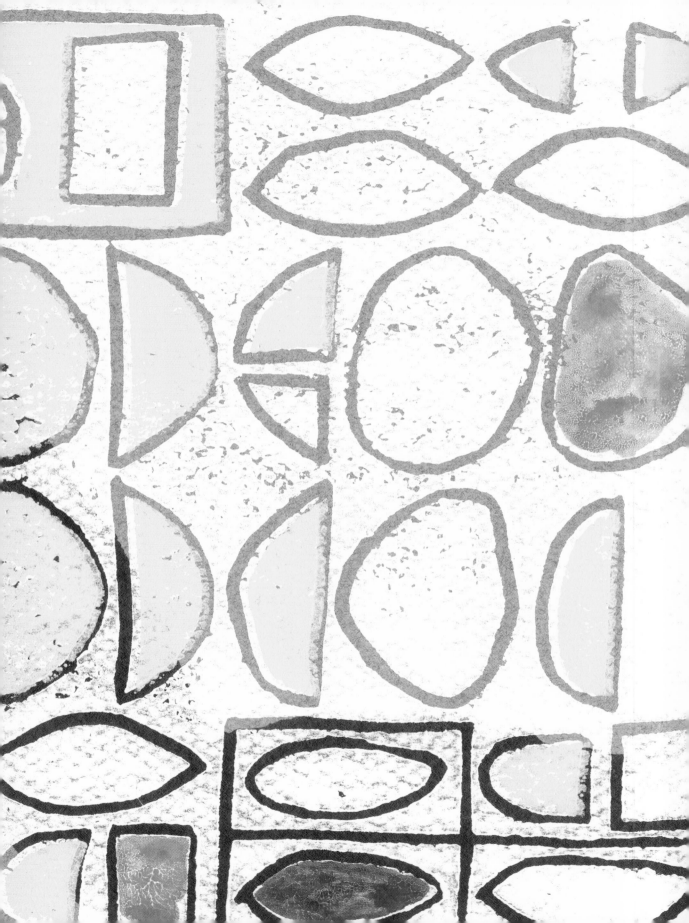

How will your inner artist nurture these treasures?

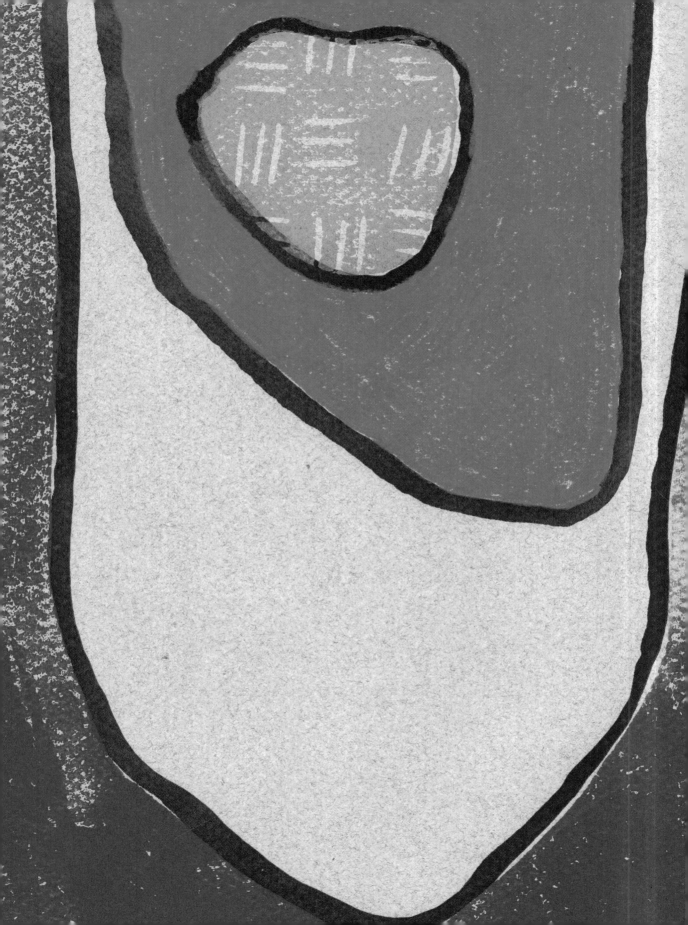

Make a list that is also a time capsule.
What are the songs, poems, art, books, movies, or plays
that speak to this period for you?

the thing I came for:
the wreck and not the story of the wreck
the thing itself and not the myth
the drowned face always staring

~toward the sun
the evidence of damage

worn by salt and sway into this threadbare beauty
the ribs of disaster
                    curving their   assertion
among the tentative haunters

diving into the wreck
adrienne rich
1973

If you were told that starting today your life will never be the same and you have the chance to start something all over, what would you do?

In some way, on this piece of paper, start doing it.

Published in 2018 by Dottir Press
33 Fifth Avenue
New York, NY 10003

Dottirpress.com

FIRST EDITION

First printing September 2018
Illustration and design by Nicole Skibola
Production by Drew Stevens

This book is typeset in Garamond. The title type and the poem on page 63
were hand lettered by Nicole. The drawing on page 63 contains a stanza
from "Diving Into the Wreck," from Adrienne Rich's poetry collection
Diving Into the Wreck, published by W.W. Norton in 1973. Copyright
© 1973 by Adrienne Rich.

Library of Congress Cataloging-in-Publication Data is available for this title.
ISBN 978-1-948340-01-4